Machines with Power!
Ships

by Amy McDonald

BELLWETHER MEDIA
MINNEAPOLIS, MN

Blastoff! Beginners are developed by literacy experts and educators to meet the needs of early readers. These engaging informational texts support young children as they begin reading about their world. Through simple language and high frequency words paired with crisp, colorful photos, Blastoff! Beginners launch young readers into the universe of independent reading.

Blastoff! Universe

Reading Level — Grade K — Blastoff! Beginners

Grades 1-3 — Blastoff! Readers

Grade 4 — Blastoff! Discovery

Sight Words in This Book 🔍

a	has	look	people	to
all	here	make	see	water
are	in	of	the	
big	is	on	they	
go	it	out	this	

This edition first published in 2021 by Bellwether Media, Inc.

No part of this publication may be reproduced in whole or in part without written permission of the publisher. For information regarding permission, write to Bellwether Media, Inc., Attention: Permissions Department, 6012 Blue Circle Drive, Minnetonka, MN 55343.

Library of Congress Cataloging-in-Publication Data

Names: McDonald, Amy, author.
Title: Ships / Amy McDonald.
Description: Minneapolis, Minnesota : Bellwether Media, 2021. | Series: Machines with power! | Includes bibliographical references and index. | Audience: Ages PreK-2 | Audience: Grades K-1
Identifiers: LCCN 2020029185 (print) | LCCN 2020029186 (ebook) | ISBN 9781644873700 (library binding) | ISBN 9781648340710 (ebook)
Subjects: LCSH: Ships--Juvenile literature.
Classification: LCC VM150 .M43 2021 (print) | LCC VM150 (ebook) | DDC 623.82--dc23
LC record available at https://lccn.loc.gov/2020029185
LC ebook record available at https://lccn.loc.gov/2020029186

Text copyright © 2021 by Bellwether Media, Inc. BLASTOFF! BEGINNERS and associated logos are trademarks and/or registered trademarks of Bellwether Media, Inc.

Editor: Christina Leaf   Designer: Andrea Schneider

Printed in the United States of America, North Mankato, MN.

Table of Contents

What Are Ships?

Look out to sea.
See the ship?

Ships are
big machines.
They travel
in water.

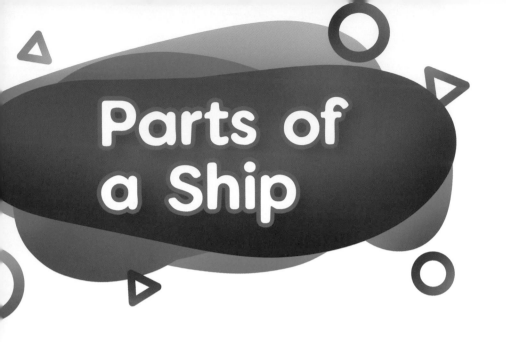

Parts of a Ship

This is the **hull**.
It is the body
of the ship.

hull

This is the **deck**.
People walk here.

deck

This is the
propeller.
It makes
the ship go.

propeller

13

Ships at Work

This ship carries **cargo**. It moves things across the sea.

cargo

This ship
carries juice.
It is a tanker.

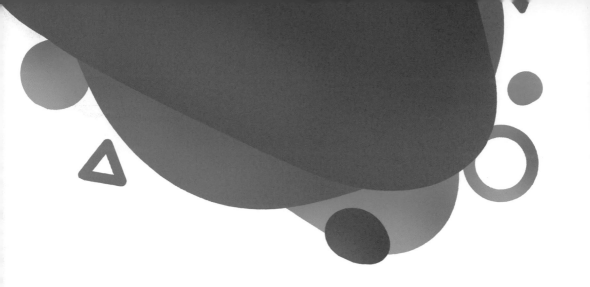

This ship has
a big deck.
Planes land on it!

plane

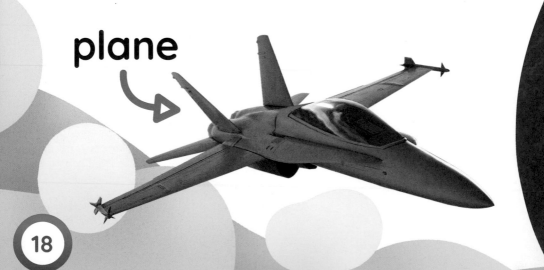

This fun ship carries people. All aboard!

Ship Facts

Ship Parts

propeller

deck

hull

Types of Ships

cargo ship

tanker

aircraft carrier

Glossary

cargo

things a ship carries

deck

a floor on a ship

hull

a ship's body

propeller

the part that pushes a ship

To Learn More

ON THE WEB

FACTSURFER

Factsurfer.com gives you a safe, fun way to find more information.

1. Go to www.factsurfer.com.

2. Enter "ships" into the search box and click 🔍.

3. Select your book cover to see a list of related content.

The images in this book are reproduced through the courtesy of: mariakray, front cover; Olga Gavrilova, p. 3; Darryl Brooks, pp. 4-5; Federico Rostagno, pp. 6-7; Aun Photographer, pp. 8-9; Vintagepix, pp. 10-11; Tawansak, pp. 12-13; Maha Heang 245789, p. 14 (cargo); ValdSV, pp. 14-15; Valery121283, p. 16 (oranges); Martin Witte/ Alamy, pp. 16-17; EmiliaUngur, p. 18 (plane); Avigator Fortuner, pp. 18-19, 23 (cargo); Denis Belitsky, pp. 20-21; Nightman1965, p. 22 (parts, cargo ship, tanker); DOGMAge, p. 22 (propeller); Joris van Boven, p. 22 (aircraft carrier); LeeYiuTung, p. 23 (deck); Andrea Izzotti, p. 23 (hull); SanerG, p. 23 (propeller).